# The BAKEWARE COOKBOOK

Must-Make Recipes for Your Favorite Bakeware

by Rochelle Palermo

*To my husband, Michael Torres*

# FOREWORD

by Curtis Stone

There's something pretty exhilarating about baking. The fragrances that fill the home, the anticipation of revealing golden deliciousness from the oven, and the excitement of digging into that warm, bubbly goodness satisfy all the senses. It's clearly something we do as a loving act for others, as much as for ourselves. Now that I have two young growing boys, I find myself in the kitchen baking sweet little treats to tuck into their lunch boxes. I always envision their faces as they open these goodies, and hope my treats serve as simple reminders of my love.

It is this joy of both cooking and baking, and sharing with others, that led me to develop Dura-Bake bakeware, an extension of my Dura-Pan cookware line. As with all my products, it is my great desire to come up with solutions to the problems most home cooks face, so that they have the confidence to cook and bake, and can reap the rewards and special memories that come with it.

When it came to putting together a companion cookbook for my bakeware, I automatically turned to my right hand in the kitchen, Rochelle Palermo. I've said it before and I'll say it again: Rochelle is the best damn baker and the queen bee in the kitchen.

I've had the pleasure of working with Rochelle since my *Take Home Chef* days, and I can tell you that she never ceases to amaze me. Her attention to detail and incredible work ethic, combined with her creativity, knowledge, love of food, and constant pursuit of perfection, make her the ideal person to bring you these recipes. And trust me, you'll want to make her recipes for your family and friends for years to come... in particular, her free-form peach and cherry pies (page 21) are not to be missed.

Rochelle is easily excitable when it comes to food, and her passion for sharing good food comes through in these pages. She knows just how to create recipes for the home cook, using easy-to-find ingredients and streamlined, simplified steps that make cooking fuss-free and fun. She takes you beyond the sweet treats of baking and into the land of sheet-pan suppers and holiday meals, and along the way creatively shows you plenty of innovative techniques for making the most of your favorite bakeware. Serving salad on a sheet pan? Mark my words, it's soon to become a thing!

"Make it great!" is all I needed to tell her. And as you can see, she's done just that.

# THANKS

This is the first cookbook I've authored, so you can imagine how exciting it is for me. I thank God each and every day for the opportunity to do work that I love and for the talented people I get to work with. This book was created with lots of heart and soul by the most exceptional people I know in the culinary world, to whom I am forever grateful.

Hands down, I would not have had this incredible opportunity if it were not for the generosity of Curtis Stone. I'm so thankful. You have such a big heart, and I seriously can't count all the opportunities you've given me and all the professional goals I've been able to achieve because of you. You're the best in the biz and I learn so much from you. It's always an honor to support you and work with you.

This project simply would not have been as pleasurable without the support of my loving husband, Michael Torres! Whenever I have working weekends, deadlines, or late nights, you're not far from my side, cheering me on, lending a hand, or offering heartfelt advice and much-needed shoulder rubs. I'm not sure what I've done to deserve such a perfect husband, but I love you with all my heart.

Thank you to my mom, dad, and grandmothers for nurturing my love of food and teaching me how to cook ever since I could reach the kitchen counter. Respect and love for food has always been at the core of our family and a topic that excited us all, and something I figured was universal but later learned was unusual (turns out most families don't plan their next meal only moments after finishing the previous one). Thank you for your never-ending encouragement, support, guidance, and love.

When you're lucky enough to work with a team of smart, hard-working, passionate food professionals, as I do, you're able to achieve really great results—a book like this is just one example. Matthew Glasser, your parents must be incredibly proud of you. What a clever, kind, and talented chef you are. Your impressive breadth of culinary knowledge, daily passion for good food, and sense of humor make you a delight to be around. Thank you for your thoughtful and trustworthy advice. Vannessa Garcia, you had me at hello with that lemon butter from the very first menu at Maude. It was a real treat to have you join our culinary team, no pun intended. Thank you for bringing fine-dining caliber to absolutely everything you do. Jenifer Gomez, as Curtis likes to say, "What can't you do?" You're a lady of many talents—too many to list here, but let's just start with my two favorites: crafting and swing dancing. Avette Aumentado, you're an absolute pleasure to work with, and there's never any doubt about your workmanship and the numerous contributions you bring to our small but mighty team. Thanks to all the Stone's Food peeps in and out of the test kitchen! Life is never dull at 6600 Sunset Boulevard.

Nathan Hinz, I knew from the first time we worked together that I would definitely be working with you again. You're incredibly talented, combining artistry and professionalism, and you make work both fun and productive. Now, can you pretty please use your funny voice when critiquing images...you know, the one that gives me the church giggles? But seriously, thank you for designing such a beautiful book, from the cover and layout right on down to the typography and paper selection. You've gone above and beyond helping me print and publish this book, and I simply can't thank you enough. Special thanks to Tracy Hogenson for your eagle eyes on layouts.

Ray Kachatorian, how many years has it been? And how many projects have we worked on together? You are family! And you're a wizard with the camera. Your ability to capture the beautiful things in life puts me in a total tailspin. Thank you for taking such gorgeous photos of my recipes that, let's face it, are what inspire us all to get into the kitchen. Great Dane and Mario— thanks for being such a super support to my man Ray.

Vivian Lui, you're a true food artist. There's no other name for you. Your way of creating beautiful food is unmatched. Your attention to detail is beyond impressive. You're the food stylist I always wished I could be. I'm so grateful to you for sharing your talents and knowledge with me. Go Bruins!

Suzie Myers, may I come live in your pretty world? I've admired your work in *Food & Wine* magazine for years! Your tasteful selection of one-of-a-kind platters, plates, glassware, utensils, fabrics, and surfaces has created the most lovely, inviting places on each page of this book, and a world that I would happily dance in forever. What a delight it has been to work with you and Nico Sherman.

Amy Steinberg, you're much more than the grammar guru I've had the pleasure of knowing since our *Bon Appétit* days. You're one of the best friends a gal can have. Thanks for your sound advice on this book and throughout the years, and always reminding me how to keep a balance in life—even when the to-do list is long— with a hike in the mountains or a stroll along the beach.

Harry Pourounidis, Jeff Norling, Sara Armstrong, Lindsey Sandvik, Gary Drain, Sonia Simmons, and Amanda Serra—both past and present Food Fighters who've worked painstakingly to bring to life the cookware, bakeware, and tools that are smart, useful, and of the highest quality—a big high five to you all. Special thanks to Jeff, Gary, and Sara for all the extra teamwork on this book!

And last, but certainly not least, a big warm cozy hug of gratitude goes to Adam Marland, Liz Gibaldi and the entire HSN family. Adam, I'm fortunate to learn so much from you. Thank you for your invaluable guidance, your sincere and straightforward critiques, and always striving to make Curtis a success. And how did we get so lucky to work with Lovely Liz? Liz, you are a joy to work with and I'm sincerely grateful for your contagious enthusiasm and delightful collaboration. Eric Tochterman, Amanda Rice, Cat Chancey, Jen Stewart, Carlos Ramos, Carmela Macahuachi, Rene Cruz, and Gayle Andrews—we've been through the trenches together in the crazy world of live television and you already know how much I absolutely love and treasure you all. To Stephanie Weeks, April McCall, Soraya Ferrari, and Andres Gomez, thank you for your expert advice and thoughtful collaboration.

There's no mistaking that we are all one big hungry, happy team.

# CONTENTS

# SHORTCUTS, TIPS, AND USES

# SHORTCUTS

*I'm so happy to be sharing my favorite recipes in this book, and I hope you'll enjoy making and eating them as much as I do. But please know that it's totally fine with me if you take a few shortcuts along the way (you'll see that I've taken quite a few myself throughout the book). Just please promise me that you'll make something!*

*Here are a few ideas to shortcut your way into baking something special.*

### Flaky Dough

Phyllo dough and puff pastry dough are your friends! You'll find them in the frozen food section of most supermarkets. If you come across a puff pastry made with all butter, stock your freezer with it; that all-butter variety makes a world of difference with its rich, delicious flavor. I've included some of my favorite uses for these pastry doughs, but the ways of using them are endless. Pinterest it!

### Pizza Dough

Today supermarkets offer more options than ever before. Look for pizza dough that you just press into the pan to make semi-scratch and utterly delicious pizza at home. Is there anything more satisfying than freshly baked bread smothered with marinara and molten cheese (a.k.a. pizza)? You can find the dough in the refrigerated or frozen food section, depending on the store.

### Cake Mixes

Let's face it, some days you just won't have time to make a homemade cake batter, and you'll need to turn to a box mix for a little help. That's okay. Box mixes for cakes, brownies, breads, and cookies have improved immensely over the years. Look for ones without all the fake stuff.

### Sauces and Spices

I've provided recipes for easy vinaigrettes, sauces, and spice mixtures, all solid building blocks for great meals. But if you have a favorite off the shelf, go right ahead and use it.

# TIPS

*You'll find tips scattered throughout the recipes, but I wanted to provide a few here that will help you make the most of all your baking, roasting, braising, and steaming time.*

### Pans

I've created all the recipes in this book using only Dura-Bake bakeware. To me, there truly is nothing better. The superior nonstick coating (over the entire pan, top and bottom!) makes food release and cleanup quick and easy. The ideal weight and durable construction promote even heat distribution, ensuring perfect golden browning. Of course, they are comparable in size to standard bakeware, so you can use Dura-Bake pans for any recipe calling for the same size pan.

### Flour

I call for unbleached flours, since I like to use foods that are processed as little as possible. But feel free to use bleached flour, if you'd like. What's the difference? Bleached flour is, well, bleached with chemical agents to speed up aging, whereas unbleached flour is bleached naturally as it ages. The difference in your baked goods will be minimal.

Cake flour, however, is considerably different from all-purpose flour and bread flour. Basically, using cake flour is crucial for delicate cakes and muffins with a tender crumb. Using bread flour, on the other hand, will result in the most delicious chewy pizza crust. Use the flour specifically called for in each recipe, for the best results. These flours can be found in the baking aisle of supermarkets.

### Butter

While the Dura-Bake nonstick surface offers superior release, go ahead and coat your pans with butter for added assurance of a clean release and an extra bonus of flavor. You'll be pleased to know that you won't need to coat these pans with flour or line them with parchment paper, as you would for other pans.

### Measure Accurately

For the best results when baking, it's essential to measure accurately. So level off your cups, tablespoons, and teaspoons.

### Oven Thermometers

Do yourself a gigantic favor and get an oven thermometer. They're inexpensive and will ensure you're baking at the right temperature. I can't stress this enough. Most ovens are not properly calibrated. So the temperature inside your oven isn't always the same temperature you set your oven to.

### Cutting Baked Goods

Never use a sharp metal knife or utensil to cut food in your bakeware, as doing so will surely damage the pan. Instead, use a sturdy dough scraper or plastic knife that's designed for nonstick bakeware.

### Meats

I prefer to buy meat from reputable local sources, raised on sustainable pasture-based family farms. Meat that comes from animals humanely raised on pastures is healthier and more nutritious, so I encourage you to consider buying it, when possible. Look for signs at the meat counter that note "Global Animal Partnership" or "Certified Humane."

# GARDEN SALAD

with Spicy Thai Vinaigrette

*Serves 4*

*Make-Ahead*
Vinaigrette can be made 1 day ahead;
cover and refrigerate.

---

**$^1/_4$ cup**
Fresh lime juice

**3 tbs**
Grapeseed oil

**2 tbs**
Asian fish sauce

**2 tbs**
Finely chopped
shallot

**1 tbs**
Grated peeled fresh
ginger

**1**
Small Thai chile,
chopped (seeded if
desired)

**1 $^1/_2$ tsp**
Sugar

**2 heads**
Little Gem lettuce,
leaves separated

**3 oz**
Spring mix greens

**1**
Baby cucumber,
shaved lengthwise
with mandoline

**2**
Red-orange carrots
peeled, shaved
lengthwise with
vegetable peeler

**4 oz**
Cherry tomatoes
(assorted colors
and sizes), halved

**2**
Radishes shaved
with mandoline

**1 cup each**
(not packed) Fresh
cilantro leaves and
small mint leaves

**$^1/_3$ cup**
Small bunashimeji
mushrooms

Blend lime juice, oil, fish sauce,
shallot, ginger, chile, and sugar in
blender until smooth.

Arrange remaining ingredients
over sheet pan. Drizzle with
vinaigrette and serve.

## Icy Raspberry
# SMOOTHIE

*Serves 2*

*Make-Ahead*
Raspberries can be frozen
up to 5 days ahead.

**1 ¹/₂ cups**
(6 oz) Fresh
raspberries

**2 cups**
Ice cubes

**1 cup**
Plain yogurt

**¹/₄ cup**
Agave syrup or
honey

**¹/₄ cup**
Fresh coconut
water

**¹/₂**
Vanilla bean, seeds
scraped, or ¹/₈ tsp
vanilla extract

Place raspberries on sheet pan and
freeze 4 hours, or until firm.

Combine frozen raspberries, ice,
yogurt, syrup, and coconut water in
blender. Add vanilla seeds (discard
bean) or vanilla extract. Blend until
icy and smooth. Pour into 2 glasses
and serve.

# USES

*When most of us think of bakeware, cakes and muffins automatically come to mind. But when you really think about it, as Curtis, the team, and I did, you'll discover there are so many more uses for it, many of which are featured in the recipes.*

*Sheet pans are the workhorses of the kitchen...I seriously couldn't function without them. Their uses extend well beyond baking cookies and toasting nuts. Here are just a few to consider.*

› Arrange berries and cut fruit over the sheet pan to freeze them in a single layer for smoothies, cocktails, and lassis. Check out the Icy Raspberry Smoothie recipe on opposite page.

› Use the large surface area of your sheet pan to collect ingredients from the fridge, garden, and pantry. No more juggling bags of flour, eggs, and sugar.

› I've never liked tossing salads in deep bowls—the delicate vegetables become buried, weighed down, and soggy. Instead, I much prefer arranging the lettuces and my jewel-like veggies over a platter or one of these sheet pans and then drizzling them with dressing (see page 15).

› Load up your sheet pan with all your barbecue needs before heading outside. Think towels, tongs, salt and pepper, sauces, basting brushes, meat thermometer, timer, etc.

› Spread drained hot cooked pasta or rice over sheet pans to cool them down quickly when making pasta salad or rice salad. When blanching vegetables, strain them from the boiling water and spread them over the sheet pan to cool, rather than chilling them in ice water. Look, Ma! No more soggy pasta and veg!

› Keep your ingredients, both raw and prepped, on a sheet pan so you can move them easily and free up counter space quickly. I even place my sheet pan over the sink to extend my counter space.

› These sheet pans are pretty enough for you to put them out as serving pieces. Use one as a platter for crudités and dip, or as a cocktail tray to catch all the condensation of icy pitchers. And that turkey on the big round deep-dish pizza pan? Sexy! Having a party? Freeze scoops of assorted ice cream over the sheet pan and keep it in the freezer, then top the ice cream with whipped cream, sliced bananas, hot chocolate fudge sauce, and toasted nuts (or use your muffin pan for all these yummy toppings and more).

› You can also keep the sheet pans in the fridge as liners to catch any drips from thawing foods, sticky jars, or leaky packages.

# SHEET PANS

## AND

## PIZZA PANS

Free-Form

# PEACH AND CHERRY PIES

*Makes 8*

²/₃ cup
Granulated sugar

1 tbs
Unbleached all-purpose flour

2 tsp
Ground cinnamon

2 lb
(about 5) Ripe but firm peaches, pitted, cut into ½-inch wedges

8 oz
(about 2 cups) Fresh cherries, pitted

8 disks
All-Butter Pie Dough (page 22)

2 tbs
Heavy cream

1 ½ tbs
Coarse sanding sugar

Lightly sweetened whipped cream or vanilla ice cream, for serving

Place racks in lowest position and center of oven; preheat to 375°F.

In large bowl, mix granulated sugar, flour, and cinnamon. Fold in peaches and cherries. Set aside, tossing fruit occasionally.

Roll out each dough disk on lightly floured surface to 8 inch diameter. Arrange dough disks on 2 sheet pans.

Divide fruit mixture among dough disks. Fold dough edges over portion of filling, softly pleating edges. Cover and chill 30 minutes, or until dough is cold and firm.

Brush crusts with cream and sprinkle with sanding sugar. Bake 50 to 60 minutes, or until crusts are golden brown and filling is bubbling. If crusts begin to brown before filling bubbles, tent pies with foil. Cool slightly.

Using spatula, loosen pies from pans and transfer to plates. Serve warm or at room temperature with sweetened whipped cream or ice cream.

## All-Butter
# PIE DOUGH

*Makes*
Enough for 8 individual free-form pies

*Make-Ahead*
Dough disks can be made up to 1 day ahead and refrigerated, or frozen up to 1 month.

---

**3 cups**
Unbleached all-purpose flour

**1 tbs**
Sugar

**1 1/2 tsp**
Kosher salt

**12 oz**
(3 sticks) Very cold unsalted butter, diced

**1/2 cup**
(or more) Ice water

In food processor, mix flour, sugar, and salt. Add butter and pulse just until mixture resembles coarse meal. Drizzle 1/2 cup ice water over dough and pulse just until dough pulls away from sides of bowl (mixture will still look crumbly). Add more ice water by teaspoonfuls to moisten, if necessary.

Transfer mixture to work surface and press dough together. Divide dough into 8 equal pieces. Flatten each piece into disk and wrap each disk separately in plastic. Chill at least 1 hour and up to 1 day.

*Rochelle's Tip:*
Never knead pie dough. The more gently it's handled, the more tender and flaky it will be. This recipe will make enough pie dough for 2 large free-form pies or 1 double-crusted pie; divide the dough in half, rather than into 8 pieces.

# Pecan Shortbread
# COOKIES

**Makes**
36 cookies

**Make-Ahead**
Wrapped dough log can be frozen up to 2 weeks; thaw before slicing.

---

**8 tbs**
(1 stick) Salted butter, softened

**1/4 cup**
Granulated sugar, plus more for garnish

**2 tbs**
Powdered sugar

**1**
Large egg yolk

**1 cup**
Unbleached all-purpose flour

**1 cup**
Pecans, coarsely chopped

In large bowl, using electric mixer on medium-high speed, beat butter, sugars, and yolk 3 minutes, or until light and fluffy. Beat in flour. Mix in pecans. Form into 12-inch-long log. Wrap in plastic and refrigerate until firm.

Preheat oven to 325°F. Unwrap log and cut dough into 1/4-inch-thick slices. Arrange on 2 sheet pans.

Bake 10 to 12 minutes, or until light golden around edges and on bottom. Garnish cookies with granulated sugar.

Girly Pink

# SHEET CAKE

*Serves 24*

*Make-Ahead*
This cake is best served the day it is made.

---

**4 1/2 cups**
Powdered sugar, sifted

**1 1/4 cups**
(2½ sticks)
Unsalted butter, softened

**1/2 cup**
Freeze-dried strawberries, pulsed in clean coffee grinder to fine powder

**1/4 cup**
Whole milk

**1 tbs**
Vanilla extract

**1/4 tsp**
Almond extract

**3/4 tsp**
Salt

**1 sheet**
Vanilla Cake (see recipe), in sheet pan

Edible flowers, for garnish

In large bowl, using electric mixer on medium speed, beat sugar, butter, strawberry powder, milk, extracts, and salt 2 minutes, or until light and airy.

Spread frosting over cake and garnish with flowers. Cut into squares and serve.

*Rochelle's Tip:*
Use other freeze-dried fruit, such as raspberries or blueberries, to create different colors of frosting, naturally.

# Vanilla Cake

*Makes*
One sheet-pan cake, two 8-inch round cakes, or 24 cupcakes

*Make-Ahead*
This cake is best served the day it is made.

---

**2 1/4 cups**
Unbleached cake flour

**1 1/2 tsp**
Baking powder

**3/4 tsp**
Baking soda

**1 1/2 cups**
Sugar

**12 tbs**
(1½ sticks)
Unsalted butter, softened

**1 tsp**
Salt

**1**
Vanilla bean, split, or 1½ tsp vanilla extract

**2**
Large eggs

**1 1/4 cups**
Sour cream

Preheat oven to 350°F. Butter 1 sheet pan, two 8-inch round cake pans, or 24 muffin cups.

In medium bowl, whisk flour, baking powder, and baking soda. In large bowl, combine sugar, butter, and salt. Scrape seeds from vanilla bean into butter mixture (reserve bean for another use) or add extract. Using electric mixer on medium-high speed, beat 2 minutes. Mix in eggs 1 at a time. Mix in sour cream. Add flour mixture and mix just until blended.

Spread batter over sheet pan, or divide between cake pans or among muffin cups.

Bake 15 minutes for sheet-pan cake, 30 minutes for 8-inch cakes, or 18 minutes for cupcakes, or until tester inserted into center of cake comes out with some crumbs attached.

Transfer pan to rack and cool 5 minutes. Run silicone spatula around cake edges to loosen from pan. Unmold cake onto wire rack, if desired, and cool.

*Makes*
18 large or 36
small cookies

*Make-Ahead*
Shaped cookies can be frozen until firm, then stored airtight 1 month. Bake cookies without thawing; allow a few extra minutes to bake.

1 cup
(2 sticks) Unsalted butter, softened

1 cup
Granulated sugar

¾ cup
Packed golden brown sugar

2 oz
Almond paste

2 tsp
Vanilla extract

½ tsp
Kosher salt

2
Large eggs

2 cups
Unbleached all-purpose flour

1 tsp
Baking soda

12 oz
Dark chocolate (60% cacao), chopped, or chocolate chips

2 cups
Walnuts or macadamia nuts, toasted, coarsely chopped

Position racks in top third and center of oven and preheat to 375°F.

In large bowl, using electric mixer on medium-high speed, beat butter, sugars, almond paste, vanilla, and salt 4 minutes, or until creamy. Beat in eggs 1 at a time. Reduce mixer speed to low and gradually add flour and baking soda, beating just until blended. Stir in chocolate and nuts.

Using about ⅓ cup dough for each large cookie or ¼ cup dough for each small cookie, drop dough onto 2 sheet pans, spacing evenly and placing 6 large cookies or 9 small cookies on each sheet pan.

Bake cookies, switching pans from top to bottom and front to back halfway through baking, for 13 minutes, or until edges and tops are golden brown but centers are still soft and moist.

Cool on pans 5 minutes. Transfer cookies to racks. Repeat with remaining dough. Serve warm.

*Rochelle's Tip:*
You can make two giant cookie cakes with this recipe. Press the dough into two 8-inch round cake pans and bake at 375°F for about 25 minutes.

# Dark
# CHOCOLATE
# CHUNK COOKIES

with **Toasted Nuts**

# HAZELNUT CRUNCH

*Makes*
About 1½ lb

*Make-Ahead*
Can be made 2 days ahead in dry climate; store airtight at room temperature.

1 ½ cups
Sugar

1 cup
Water

½ cup
Organic light corn syrup

⅓ cup
Pure maple syrup

2 ½ cups
Skinned toasted hazelnuts, coarsely chopped

2 tbs
Unsalted butter

½ tsp
Salt

1 tsp
Baking soda

In large saucepan over medium heat, stir sugar, water, corn syrup, and maple syrup until sugar dissolves. Increase heat to high and boil without stirring 10 minutes, or until instant-read thermometer registers 260°F.

Reduce heat to medium-low. Mix in hazelnuts, butter, and salt and stir 10 minutes, or until thermometer registers 295°F.

Quickly mix in baking soda and pour over sheet pan, spreading thinly. Let stand until hard.

Break into pieces and store in airtight container at room temperature.

Rosemary–Sea Salt

# FLATBREAD CRACKERS

**Makes**
About 36

**Make-Ahead**
Can be made up to 3 days ahead; store airtight at room temperature.

**1 ¼ cups**
Finely grated Parmesan cheese, divided

**¾ cup**
Unbleached all-purpose flour

**1 tsp**
Chopped fresh rosemary

**¼ tsp**
Baking powder

**½ tsp**
Sea salt

**3 tbs**
Extra-virgin olive oil, divided

Preheat oven to 325°F. In food processor, blend 1 cup cheese, flour, rosemary, baking powder, and salt. Add ¼ cup water and 2 tbs oil; pulse to form dough.

Invert sheet pan on work surface. Roll out dough over back of sheet pan to cover surface completely. Coat with remaining oil and cheese. Using fork, pierce dough all over.

Bake 20 to 22 minutes, or until pale golden. Cool completely on sheet pan, then break into about thirty-six 3x2-inch pieces.

Crunchy

# ROASTED POTATOES

*Serves 4 - 6*

*Make-Ahead*

Potatoes can be steamed 2 days ahead, then cooled, covered, and chilled. Add 5 minutes to roasting time before adding butter, rosemary, and garlic.

**3 lb**
Yukon Gold potatoes, peeled, halved lengthwise, then cut on diagonal into 2-inch pieces

**3 tbs**
Olive oil

**1 ¹/₂ tsp**
Kosher salt

**3 tbs**
Butter

**6 sprigs**
Fresh rosemary

**6 cloves**
Garlic

**1 tbs**
Finely chopped fresh parsley

Preheat oven to 450°F. On sheet pan, arrange potatoes in even layer. Place pan in oven and pour 3 cups water over. Invert second sheet pan in offset position over pan of potatoes to mostly cover potatoes.

Bake 30 minutes, or until potatoes are tender. Transfer potatoes to colander to drain water. Meanwhile, transfer empty sheet pan to oven.

In colander, toss potatoes with oil and 1 ¹/₂ tsp kosher salt. Transfer potatoes to preheated sheet pan in oven. Roast uncovered 30 minutes, or until potatoes are crisp all over.

Scatter butter, rosemary, and garlic all around potatoes and shake pan to coat potatoes. Roast 15 minutes longer. Toss potatoes with parsley and season with salt and pepper.

*Serves 6 - 8*

*Make-Ahead*
Layered phyllo can be baked up to 2 days
ahead; store airtight at room temperature.

**7**
14x9-inch sheets
phyllo pastry, thawed
if frozen

**7 tbs**
Butter, melted

**7 tbs**
Finely grated
Parmesan cheese
(about 2 oz)

**5 oz**
Goat cheese

**1/4 cup**
Plain Greek yogurt

**8 oz**
Heirloom tomatoes
(assorted colors and
sizes), thinly sliced
crosswise

**3 tbs**
Extra-virgin olive oil

**1**
Lemon, zest finely
grated, juiced

**1 tbs**
Finely chopped
shallot

**2 tbs each**
Fresh basil leaves
and small mint leaves

Preheat oven to 325°F.

Lay 1 phyllo sheet over sheet pan.
Brush with butter and sprinkle
with 1 tbs Parmesan. Repeat
layering with remaining phyllo
sheets, brushing each with butter
and sprinkling each with 1 tbs
Parmesan. Pierce pastry all over
with fork.

Bake 18 to 20 minutes, or until
deep golden, occasionally pressing
pastry with spatula. Cool. Transfer
phyllo to large platter.

In large bowl, using electric mixer
on medium-high speed, beat goat
cheese and yogurt until fluffy; spread
over phyllo. Top with tomatoes.

Whisk oil, 2 tbs lemon juice,
2 tsp lemon zest, and shallot
to blend. Season with salt and
pepper. Drizzle some dressing
over tomatoes. Sprinkle basil
and mint over tart. Cut and serve
immediately with more dressing.

# PHYLLO TART

with **Backyard Tomatoes** and **Feta Yogurt**

# PARTY LASAGNA

*Serves 12*

*Make-Ahead*
Lasagna can be assembled, covered, and refrigerated up to 1 day ahead before baking.

1 tbs
Extra-virgin olive oil

5 cups
Simple Marinara
Sauce (page 36) or
purchased

18 sheets
No-boil dried lasagna
noodles

6 cups
Grated whole-milk
mozzarella cheese
(about 1 lb)

3/4 cup
Freshly grated
Parmesan cheese
(preferably
Parmigiano-
Reggiano)

2 cups
Béchamel Sauce
(page 37)

Position rack in top third of oven and preheat to 450°F. Brush sheet pan with oil.

Spoon 1 1/4 cups marinara sauce over sheet pan. Line bottom with 6 pasta noodles. Spread evenly with 1 1/4 cups marinara, then sprinkle with 2 cups mozzarella cheese and 1/4 cup Parmesan cheese. Spread 1 cup béchamel sauce over. Top with 6 noodles, spread with 1 1/4 cups marinara, then sprinkle with 2 cups mozzarella cheese and 1/4 cup Parmesan. Spread 1 cup béchamel sauce over. Repeat to form 1 more layer of noodles and spread with remaining 1 1/4 cups marinara. Cover sheet pan tightly with foil.

Bake 35 minutes, or until noodles are tender. Uncover and sprinkle 2 cups mozzarella and 1/4 cup Parmesan over lasagna. Bake 15 minutes longer, or until cheese has melted and browned. Rest 10 minutes before serving.

# SIMPLE MARINARA SAUCE

*Makes*
6 cups

*Make-Ahead*
Can be made 2 days ahead; cover and refrigerate.

---

$1/4$ cup
Extra-virgin olive oil

10 cloves
Garlic, chopped
(about ¼ cup
chopped garlic)

2 tbs
Tomato paste

2 tsp
Kosher salt

1 tsp
Dried oregano

$1/2$ tsp
Crushed red pepper
flakes

Two 26-oz cans
Crushed tomatoes
(preferably organic
San Marzano
tomatoes)

In large saucepan over medium-low heat, heat oil. Add garlic and sauté 5 minutes, or until pale golden. Stir in tomato paste, salt, oregano, and red pepper flakes; cook 2 minutes. Add tomatoes and $3/4$ cup water.

Bring to simmer. Simmer gently, stirring occasionally, for 15 minutes.

# BÉCHAMEL SAUCE

*Makes*
3 cups

*Make-Ahead*
Can be made 2 days ahead; cover and refrigerate.

2 cups
Heavy cream

2 cups
Whole milk

4 tbs
(½ stick) Unsalted butter

¼ cup
Unbleached all-purpose flour

In medium saucepan over medium heat, heat cream and milk until hot but not simmering.

Meanwhile, in large saucepan over medium-low heat, melt butter. Add flour and cook, stirring, 5 minutes, or until smooth paste forms. Gradually whisk in hot milk mixture until smooth. Bring sauce to a boil. Cook 10 minutes, stirring constantly. Season with salt.

*Rochelle's Tip:*
Think of this as a homemade replacement for canned creamed soup that can be used in your baked casseroles, such as chicken pot pies, mac and cheese, and everyone's favorite: green bean casserole.

*Serves 4*

*Make-Ahead*
Ginger-soy sauce can be made up to
1 day ahead; cover and refrigerate.

**4 fillets**
Skinless salmon
(6 oz each)

**2 tbs**
Olive oil, divided

**12 oz**
Broccolini

**1/3 cup**
Soy sauce

**1 1/2 tbs**
Fresh lemon juice

**1/2 tsp**
Toasted sesame oil

**1-inch piece**
Fresh ginger, peeled

**1 1/2 cups**
Freshly steamed
brown rice, for
serving

**1 tbs**
Sesame seeds,
toasted

Place rack in lowest position in
oven and preheat to 450°F.

Coat salmon with 1/2 tbs oil and
toss broccolini with 1 1/2 tbs oil.
Season salmon and broccolini
with salt and place on sheet pan.
Bake, turning broccolini over
occasionally, for 12 to 15 minutes,
or until broccolini is crisp-tender
and browned in spots and salmon
is mostly opaque, with rosy center.

Meanwhile, in small serving bowl,
whisk soy sauce, lemon juice, and
sesame oil. Using fine grater, grate
ginger into soy mixture.

Divide rice, salmon, and broccolini
among plates. Sprinkle with
sesame seeds and serve with
ginger-soy sauce.

15-Minute Oven-Roasted

# SALMON AND BROCCOLINI

with Ginger-Soy Sauce

Charred

# RAJAS AND SHRIMP TACOS

*Serves 4*

*Make-Ahead*
These are best served right away.

1 each
Red, orange, and yellow bell peppers, seeded, cut into ½-inch-wide strips

4
Poblano chiles, seeded, cut into ½-inch-wide strips

1
Large red onion, cut into ½-inch wide strips

5 cloves
Garlic, chopped

¼ cup
Olive oil

1½ lb
Jumbo or extra-large shrimp, peeled, deveined

*Accompaniments:*
8 warm corn tortillas, sour cream, cilantro, lemon wedges, hot sauce

Preheat oven to 450°F. In large bowl, toss peppers, chiles, onion, garlic, and oil to coat. Divide between 2 sheet pans. Season with salt. Roast, stirring occasionally, for 30 minutes, or until tender. Fold in shrimp, scraping pan with silicon spatula. Roast 5 minutes, or until shrimp are just cooked through. Season with salt.

Divide shrimp mixture among tortillas. Top with sour cream and cilantro. Serve with lemon wedges and hot sauce.

*Serves 4*

*Make-Ahead*
The pico de gallo can be made 1 hour ahead; cover and refrigerate.

**6**
Boneless skinless chicken thighs, each cut into 4 pieces

**4 tbs**
Extra-virgin olive oil, divided

**1 clove**
Garlic, minced

**1 1/4 tsp each**
Ground cumin and paprika

**4**
Pita breads or flatbreads

**8 oz**
Cherry tomatoes (assorted colors and sizes), quartered

**2**
Baby cucumbers, diced

**2**
Radishes, diced

**1/2 cup**
Fresh mint leaves, chopped

**2**
Green onions, chopped

**1**
Jalapeño chile, seeded, finely chopped

**2 tbs**
Fresh lemon juice

Position rack in top third of oven and preheat to 450°F.

In large bowl, toss chicken, 2 tbs oil, garlic, cumin, and paprika. Season with salt and pepper. Thread chicken onto 8 small metal skewers. Arrange skewers on sheet pan and roast, turning as needed, for 25 minutes, or until cooked through. Warm pitas alongside sheet pan, turning as needed, during last 2 minutes, or until hot and beginning to crisp.

Meanwhile, toss tomatoes, cucumbers, radishes, mint, green onions, chile, lemon juice, and 2 tbs oil. Season with salt. Top pitas with chicken and pico de gallo.

# CHICKEN SKEWERS

with Cucumber Pico and Flatbread

# ROASTED CHICKEN AND CAULIFLOWER

with Israeli Couscous

*Serves 4*

*Make-Ahead*
The Israeli couscous can be cooked, then covered and refrigerated up to 2 days. Bring to room temperature before using.

**2 tbs**
Olive oil, divided

**1 tbs**
Fennel seeds, coarsely crushed

**4**
Chicken leg quarters

**1 head**
Cauliflower, separated into large florets

**1 cup**
Dried Israeli couscous

**2 tbs**
Extra-virgin olive oil

**2 tbs**
Chopped fresh parsley

**1**
Lemon, zest finely grated, juiced

**2 cups**
(not packed) Wild arugula

Preheat oven to 450°F. In small bowl, combine 1 tbs olive oil, fennel seeds, 1 tsp salt, and $1/2$ tsp pepper. Coat chicken with spice mixture. Place chicken, skin side up, on sheet pan or deep-dish pizza pan. Roast 30 minutes.

In large bowl, toss cauliflower with 1 tbs oil and sprinkle with salt. Add cauliflower to sheet pan alongside chicken. Roast 15 minutes, or until chicken is cooked through and cauliflower is slightly charred and crisp-tender.

Meanwhile, in large saucepan of boiling salted water, cook couscous 7 minutes, or until al dente. Drain well and spread couscous over second sheet pan to cool slightly. Toss couscous with extra-virgin olive oil, parsley, lemon zest, and lemon juice and season with salt and pepper. Add roasted cauliflower and arugula and toss to combine. Top with chicken.

Pour off and discard fat from sheet pan that chicken was roasted on. Add $1/2$ cup boiling water to sheet pan and, using wooden spatula, scrape up browned bits on bottom of hot pan. Strain into serving bowl, season with salt and pepper, and serve alongside chicken.

*Serves 6 - 8*

*Make-Ahead*
The beef can be slow-cooked to 120°F and
held in a warm place for up to 1 hour before
searing in a hot oven.

---

**1**
(3-rib) Standing
rib roast of beef
(6 to 8 lb), room
temperature

**1 tbs**
Olive oil

**1 1/2 cups**
Beef stock

**2 sprigs**
Fresh thyme

Preheat oven to 225°F. Place beef
on sheet pan or deep-dish pizza
pan. Coat beef with oil and season
generously with salt and pepper.

Roast beef until instant-read
thermometer inserted into center
of meat (do not touch bone)
registers 120°F for rare doneness,
3 to 3 1/2 hours, depending on size
of roast. Set beef aside on plate and
pour off accumulated fat in pan.
Reserve fat and use for Yorkshire
puddings or discard.

Increase oven temperature to
450°F. Return beef to pan and
place in oven. Roast 10 minutes, or
until deeply browned. Transfer beef
to carving board to rest 15 minutes
before carving and serving.

Meanwhile, in small saucepan,
bring beef stock and thyme to boil.
Add hot stock to hot sheet pan and,
using wooden spatula, scrape up
browned bits on bottom of pan.
Strain into serving bowl and season
beef jus with salt and pepper.

Cut ribs from roast, cut meat into
1/2-inch-thick slices, and serve
with beef jus.

Matt's Slow-Roasted

# PRIME BEEF RIB

with Beef Jus

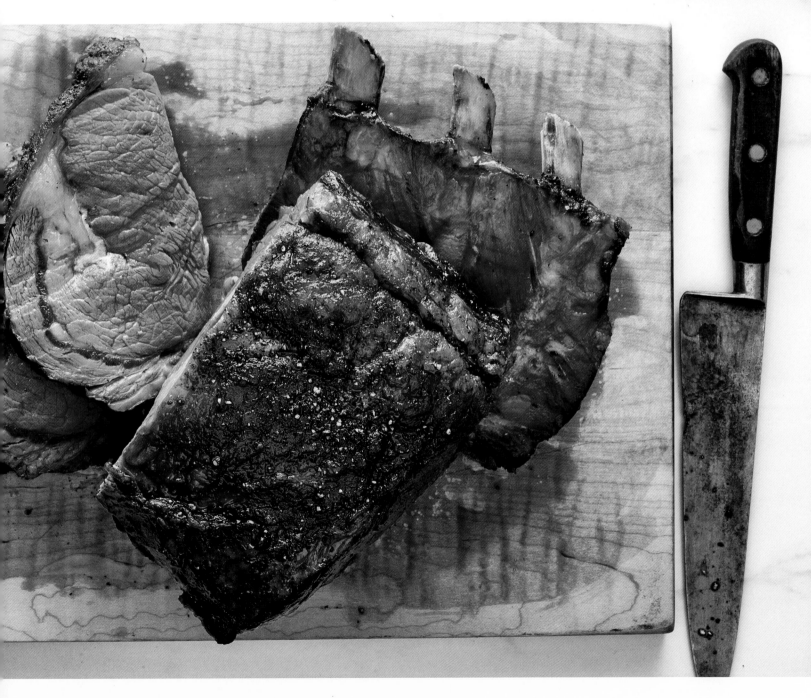

# Game-Day STEAK SANDWICHES

### with Cornichon-Shallot Relish

*Serves 12*

*Make-Ahead*

The relish can be made up to 4 hours ahead; cover and refrigerate.

---

**24**
Cornichons, shaved lengthwise (about 1 cup)

**1 cup**
Shaved shallots

**1/2 cup**
Chopped fresh parsley

**2**
Lemons, zest finely grated, juiced

**2 cloves**
Garlic, shaved

**1/2 cup + 3 tbs**
Extra-virgin olive oil, divided

**3**
Baguettes, each split and quartered

Matt's Slow-Roasted Prime Beef Rib with Beef Jus (page 46), freshly cooked, warm, thinly sliced

In medium bowl, mix cornichons, shallots, parsley, lemon zest, lemon juice, garlic, and 1/2 cup oil. Season with salt and pepper and set relish aside.

Preheat broiler. Place baguette pieces, cut side up, on sheet pan and brush with 3 tbs oil. Place under broiler 1 to 2 minutes, or until golden brown.

Place prime rib slices over baguette bottoms. Drizzle with some beef jus and sprinkle with salt and pepper. Spoon relish over sandwiches. Cover with baguette tops and serve.

*Rochelle's Tip:*
Use the deep-dish pizza pan as a serving tray for these sandwiches.

*Serves 6*

*Make-Ahead*
The pork and the corn are
best eaten hot from the oven.

**2 tbs**
Paprika

**1 1/2 tbs**
Kosher salt

**2 tsp each**
Black pepper,
cayenne pepper,
ground cumin, and
garlic powder

**One 5-lb**
Bone-in pork
shoulder

**6 ears**
Corn, husks
removed

**1/2 cup**
Crumbled Cotija or
feta cheese

*Accompaniments:*
Warm corn tortillas,
shredded cabbage,
shaved radishes,
cilantro sprigs, pico
de gallo, guacamole,
lime wedges

Preheat oven to 300°F.

Mix spices in bowl. Coat pork with
all but 2 tsp spice mixture. Wrap
pork with foil to encase completely.
Set pork on sheet pan or in deep-
dish pizza pan and roast 5 hours,
or until meat is fork-tender. Pour
off pan juices; spoon off fat and
reserve juices.

Increase oven temperature to 450°F.
Return pork to sheet pan without
foil. Coat corn with pan juices and
arrange around pork. Roast pork
and corn 30 minutes, or until pork
and corn are nicely browned.

Sprinkle corn with cheese and 2
tsp spice mixture. Serve pork and
corn with accompaniments.

*Rochelle's Tip:*
Hey, this pan is big! Plenty of space
to make an entire sheet-pan meal.
Here, the *elote* (a.k.a. Mexican
street corn) roasts right alongside
the pork.

# PORK ROAST

with Elote

# RIBS

with **North Carolina–Style Mop**

*Serves 6 - 8*

*Make-Ahead*
The baked ribs can be made up to 8 hours ahead; cool and refrigerate. Rewarm, covered, in 300°F oven.

**3 racks**
Baby back ribs (about 6 lb total)

**2 tbs**
Olive oil

**1 cup**
Apple cider vinegar

**3/4 cup**
Packed golden brown sugar

**2 tbs**
Tomato paste

**2 tsp**
Crushed red pepper flakes

**1 tsp**
Ground black pepper

**1/8 tsp**
Cayenne pepper

*Accompaniments:*
Slaw, sliced dill pickles

Preheat oven to 300°F. Line sheet pan with foil. Coat ribs with oil and season generously with salt and pepper. Place ribs, meaty side up, on prepared sheet pan and cover tightly with foil.

Bake, turning ribs over halfway, for 2 1/2 hours, or until meat is tender. Pour pan drippings into small saucepan (you should have about 1 cup). Spoon off all but about 2 tbs excess fat. Keep ribs covered. Increase oven temperature to 450°F.

To pan drippings and pork fat, add vinegar, sugar, tomato paste, red pepper flakes, black pepper, and cayenne. Simmer over medium heat, stirring occasionally, for 15 minutes, or until reduced by half. Season to taste with salt.

Brush some sauce over bony side of ribs. Bake uncovered 5 minutes. Turn ribs over and baste meaty side with sauce. Bake 10 minutes, basting every 5 minutes. Remove from oven and brush with remaining sauce.

Serve ribs with slaw and pickles.

*Serves 8*

*Make-Ahead*
The turkey can brine up to
24 hours in the refrigerator.

**6 quarts**
Cold water, divided

**1 cup**
Kosher salt

**1 cup**
Packed golden
brown sugar

**1/2 cup**
Cajun Spice Mix (see
recipe)

**2 sprigs**
Fresh rosemary

**One 14-to-16-lb**
Whole turkey

**2**
Onions, coarsely
chopped

**2**
Green bell peppers,
coarsely chopped

**3**
Celery stalks,
coarsely chopped

**12 tbs**
(1½ sticks) Unsalted
butter, divided

**3 cups (about)**
Reduced-sodium
chicken stock

**1/4 cup**
Unbleached all-
purpose flour

*To brine turkey:*
In large pot, bring 1 quart water
to boil over high heat. Add salt,
sugar, and 1/3 cup Cajun spice
mix and stir until sugar dissolves.
Add rosemary sprigs and remove
from heat.

Pour mixture into container large
enough to hold turkey, add 5 quarts
cold water, and set aside to cool.
Submerge turkey in cooled brine.
Cover and refrigerate for at least
12 hours.

*To roast turkey:*
Preheat oven to 350°F.

Remove turkey from brine and
discard brine, reserving rosemary,
then pat turkey skin dry with
towel. Stuff turkey cavity with
half each of onions, bell peppers,
and celery, and reserved rosemary
sprigs. Tie turkey legs together
with butcher's twine.

In small saucepan, melt 8 tbs
butter. Remove from heat and stir
in 2 tbs Cajun spice mix.

Place remaining onions, bell peppers,
and celery in center of 14-inch deep-
dish pizza pan or sheet pan. Place
turkey atop vegetables. Brush some
spice butter all over turkey.

*(continued on page 57)*

# ROASTED TURKEY AND PAN GRAVY

for Giving Thanks

## Continued

*To brine turkey:*
In large pot, bring 1 quart water to boil over high heat. Add salt, sugar, and 1/3 cup Cajun spice mix and stir until sugar dissolves. Add rosemary sprigs and remove from heat.

Pour mixture into container large enough to hold turkey, add 5 quarts cold water, and set aside to cool. Submerge turkey in cooled brine. Cover and refrigerate for at least 12 hours.

*To roast turkey:*
Preheat oven to 350°F.

Remove turkey from brine and discard brine, reserving rosemary, then pat turkey skin dry with towel. Stuff turkey cavity with half each of onions, bell peppers, and celery, and reserved rosemary sprigs. Tie turkey legs together with butcher's twine.

In small saucepan, melt 8 tbs butter. Remove from heat and stir in 2 tbs Cajun spice mix.

Place remaining onions, bell peppers, and celery in center of 14-inch deep-dish pizza pan or sheet pan. Place turkey atop vegetables. Brush some spice butter all over turkey.

*(continued on page 57)*

# Cajun Spice Mix

| *Makes* | *Make-Ahead* |
|---|---|
| ½ cup | Spice mix can be made 1 week ahead; store airtight at room temperature. |

2 tbs each
Garlic powder and paprika

1 tbs each
Dried oregano, thyme, black pepper, onion powder, and cayenne pepper

In small bowl, mix all ingredients to blend.

# Pizza Dough

*Makes*

*Make-Ahead*
Freeze dough balls up to 1 month. Allow extra time for the dough to rise.

1 cup
Warm water

$^1/_3$ cup
Good-quality dry white wine

1 tbs
Dry yeast

1 tbs
Honey

1 tbs
Olive oil

3 cups
Unbleached bread flour

1 $^1/_2$ tsp
Kosher salt

In 2-cup measuring cup, whisk warm water, wine, yeast, and honey to blend. Set aside 5 minutes, or until foamy. Mix in oil.

Place flour and salt in food processor. With machine running, mix in yeast mixture (dough will be wet). Transfer dough to floured work surface and knead 3 minutes, or until it is smooth, elastic, and very tacky but releases from hands.

Form dough into three balls. Place on sheet pan and dust top with flour. Cover with plastic wrap. Place dough in warm area 45 minutes, or until it rises and doubles.

*Makes*
1 pizza

*Make-Ahead*
This pizza is best eaten hot from the oven.

One 10-oz ball
Pizza Dough (see recipe) or purchased

$^1/_2$ cup
Simple Marinara Sauce (page 36) or purchased

4 oz
Fresh mozzarella cheese, torn

$^1/_4$ cup
Finely grated Parmesan cheese (preferably Parmigiano-Reggiano)

Pinch
Of crushed red pepper flakes

1 cup
(not packed) Wild arugula

4 leaves
Fresh basil, torn

2 tsp
Extra-virgin olive oil

$^1/_2$
Lemon

Flaky sea salt

Place rack in lowest position in oven and preheat oven to 450°F.

Stretch dough over perforated pizza pan. Spoon marinara sauce over dough and scatter mozzarella over. Sprinkle with Parmesan and red pepper flakes.

Bake 15 minutes, or until crust is crisp and golden brown on bottom. Transfer pizza to cutting board. Scatter arugula and basil over. Drizzle with oil, squeeze lemon juice over, and sprinkle with sea salt. Cut into wedges and serve.

*Rochelle's Tip:*
This recipe can be increased to make multiple pizzas, which I usually do, since Mike loves pizza! Long story short: Mike took my pizza class; we got married.

# PIZZA for Mike

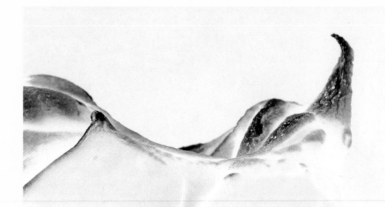

# CAKE PANS

## AND

# LOAF PANS

# YOGURT PANNA COTTA

with Blue Fruits

*Serves 8*

*Make-Ahead*
Can be made 2 days ahead; keep refrigerated.
Top with fruit and honey just before serving.

Canola oil, for
coating pan

3 tbs
Fresh lemon juice

2 $\frac{1}{2}$ tsp
Unflavored gelatin

1 $\frac{3}{4}$ cups
Heavy cream, divided

$\frac{3}{4}$ cup
Sugar

2 $\frac{1}{4}$ cups
Organic plain whole-
milk yogurt

1 small
Ripe plum, thinly sliced

$\frac{1}{2}$ cup
Fresh blackberries,
halved lengthwise

$\frac{1}{3}$ cup
Fresh blueberries

1 tbs
Honey

Lightly coat inside of 8-inch round cake pan with oil. In small bowl, combine lemon juice with 1 tbs water. Sprinkle gelatin over and stir to blend. Let stand 15 minutes to soften gelatin.

In small saucepan, combine 1 cup cream and sugar. Bring to simmer over medium heat, stirring until sugar dissolves. Remove from heat. Whisk in gelatin mixture until gelatin dissolves.

In large bowl, whisk yogurt and $\frac{3}{4}$ cup cream to blend. Whisk in cream-gelatin mixture. Transfer to prepared pan. Cover and refrigerate 8 hours, or until set.

Using small knife, cut around panna cotta to loosen edges. Fill large bowl with 1 inch of hot water. Dip bottom of pan into hot water 30 seconds to help loosen panna cotta. Dry off pan and invert panna cotta onto platter.

Scatter plum slices, blackberries, and blueberries over panna cotta. Drizzle with honey and serve.

Jen's Strawberry

# ITALIAN ICE

**Serves 6**

*Make-Ahead*
Can be made up to 5 days ahead;
cover and keep frozen.

**1 lb**
Fresh ripe
strawberries,
stemmed

**1/2 cup**
Sugar

**1/4 cup**
Fresh lemon juice

In blender, puree strawberries, sugar, lemon juice, and
2/3 cup water until smooth.

Strain strawberry puree into 8-inch round cake
pan or 9-inch square pan. Freeze 1 hour, or until icy
around edges.

Using fork, stir icy parts of puree into middle of pan.
Continue to freeze until mixture is frozen, stirring
edges into center every 30 minutes, about 3 hours.

Scrape Italian ice into flaky crystals (do not scrape
bottom of pan). Spoon into glasses and serve.

# Mom's Herb
# STUFFING

*Serves 8 - 10*

*Make-Ahead*
Unbaked stuffing can be made up to 6 hours ahead; cover and refrigerate. Add 10 minutes to baking time.

**2 lb**
Ciabatta bread, cut into ¾-inch cubes

**2 ½ sticks**
Butter, plus more for coating pans

**2 bunches**
Green onions, thinly sliced (about 3 cups)

**5 stalks**
Celery, cut into ¼-inch pieces (about 2 cups)

**1 cup**
Chopped fresh parsley

**1 ½ tbs each**
Chopped fresh oregano, sage, and thyme

**1 large clove**
Garlic, finely chopped

**3**
Large eggs, lightly beaten

**2 cups**
Reduced-sodium chicken broth

**4 oz**
Coarsely grated Parmesan cheese

Preheat oven to 350°F. Spread bread on 2 sheet pans. Bake 20 minutes, or until dry. Cool. Maintain oven temperature.

In heavy large skillet over medium heat, melt butter. Add green onions, celery, parsley, oregano, sage, thyme, and garlic; sauté 6 minutes, or until celery is tender.

Toss bread cubes and warm vegetable mixture in very large bowl. Fold in eggs and broth. Mix in cheese.

Butter two 8-inch round cake pans, two 9-inch square baking pans, or 13x9-inch baking pan. Transfer stuffing to pans. Cover with buttered foil. Bake 30 minutes. Remove foil and bake 30 minutes, or until golden.

## Sunday Mushroom-Asiago
# STRATA

*Serves 8 - 10*

*Make-Ahead*
The mushroom mixture with stock can be made up to 1 day ahead; cover and refrigerate.

---

**4 tbs**
(2 oz) Unsalted butter, plus more for coating pan

**2 cups**
(4 oz) Sliced stemmed fresh shiitake mushrooms

**1 cup**
Sliced leeks (white and pale green parts only)

**4 oz**
Ciabatta bread, cubed (about 3 cups)

**1 tbs**
Chopped fresh tarragon

**1 cup**
Reduced-sodium chicken stock

**2 cups**
Heavy cream

**6**
Large eggs

**1 cup**
Shredded Asiago cheese, divided

Preheat oven to 350°F. Butter 8-inch round cake pan or 9-inch square baking pan.

In large sauté pan over medium heat, melt butter. Add mushrooms and leeks and sauté 8 minutes, or until mushrooms are tender. Stir in bread, tarragon, 1 tsp salt, and $1/2$ tsp pepper. Stir in chicken stock and remove from heat.

In large bowl, whisk cream and eggs to blend. Stir in $2/3$ cup cheese. Fold in mushroom mixture. Transfer to prepared pan.

Sprinkle $1/3$ cup cheese over and bake uncovered 45 minutes, or until strata puffs and is golden brown on top. Cool in pan 10 minutes before serving.

# Milk Chocolate Cake

*Makes*
Two 8-inch cakes, 24 cupcakes, or 1 sheet-pan cake

*Make-Ahead*
This cake is best served the same day it's made.

*Serves 8*

*Make-Ahead*
This cake is best served the same day it's made.

---

Unsalted butter, for coating pan

²/₃ cup
Natural unsweetened cocoa powder

3 oz
High-quality milk chocolate (40% cacao), chopped

²/₃ cup
Boiling water

²/₃ cup
Buttermilk

1²/₃ cups
Unbleached cake flour

1¹/₄ tsp
Baking soda

³/₄ tsp
Kosher salt

³/₄ cup
Packed dark brown sugar

²/₃ cup
Granulated sugar

²/₃ cup
Canola oil

2
Large eggs

1¹/₂ tsp
Vanilla extract

Position rack in center of oven; preheat to 350°F. Butter two 8-inch round cake pans, 24 muffin cups, or sheet pan. In medium bowl, combine cocoa powder and milk chocolate. Pour ²/₃ cup boiling water over; whisk until mixture is smooth. Whisk in buttermilk.

In another medium bowl, whisk flour, baking soda, and salt. In large bowl, using electric mixer on medium-high speed, beat sugars, oil, eggs, and vanilla until well blended. Add flour mixture and cocoa mixture; beat until blended. Divide batter between pans.

Bake until tester inserted into center of cake comes out with some crumbs attached, about 25 minutes for 8-inch cakes, or 13 minutes for cupcakes or sheet-pan cake. Cool cakes on racks 10 minutes. Invert onto racks and cool completely.

---

8 oz
High-quality semisweet chocolate (60% cacao), chopped

8 oz
High-quality milk chocolate (40% cacao), chopped

1¹/₃ cups
Sour cream

8 tbs
(1 stick) Unsalted butter, softened

¹/₃ cup
Agave syrup

2
8-inch round Milk Chocolate Cakes (see recipe)

Edible flowers, for decorating

Place chocolates in large metal bowl. Set bowl over saucepan of simmering water and stir just until melted and smooth. Remove bowl from over water.

Add sour cream, butter, and syrup to chocolate and whisk until smooth.

Using serrated knife, cut each cake horizontally in half. Place 1 cake layer, cut side up, on platter. Spread ³/₄ cup frosting over. Top with 2 more cake layers and frosting. Top with remaining cake layer, cut side down. Spread remaining frosting over top and spread a thin layer around sides.

Decorate with flowers and serve.

*Rochelle's Tip:*
Use this rich chocolate frosting on cupcakes or on a sheet cake. It's also great on the Vanilla Cake (page 25).

Chocolate Naked
# LAYER CAKE

Parm-Crusted

# MAC AND CHEESE

*Serves 8 - 10*

*Make-Ahead*
The mac and cheese, without the panko topping, can be made 1 day ahead; cover and chill. Allow a few extra minutes cooking time.

---

**1 tbs**
Butter, softened

**1 clove**
Garlic, halved

**1 cup**
Freshly grated Parmesan cheese, divided

**1 cup**
Panko breadcrumbs

**2 tbs**
Butter, melted

**1 lb**
Cheddar cheese, shredded

**1 lb**
Conchiglie or other tube-shaped pasta

**3 cups**
Béchamel Sauce (page 37), hot

Place rack in highest position in oven; preheat to 400°F. Coat two 8-inch round cake pans or 13x9-inch baking pan with softened butter. Rub garlic over pans. Sprinkle $^1/_3$ cup Parmesan cheese over bottom and sides of pans to coat. Set aside.

In medium bowl, mix panko, melted butter, and $^1/_3$ cup Parmesan; set aside.

In large bowl, combine Cheddar cheese and $^1/_3$ cup Parmesan; set aside.

In large pot of boiling salted water, cook pasta 6 minutes, or until softened but still very firm to bite. Drain water, then pour pasta and hot béchamel sauce over cheeses in bowl. Cover and let stand 5 minutes. Stir to coat. Season with salt.

Divide between prepared pans. Sprinkle panko mixture over. Bake on top rack 10 minutes, or until heated through and golden brown on top.

# Vannessa's Lemon Butter

*Makes*
1¼ cups

*Make-Ahead*
Can be made up to 5 days ahead;
cover and refrigerate.

---

2
Large eggs

½ cup
Sugar

⅓ cup
Fresh lemon juice

5 tbs
Unsalted butter,
diced, softened

In medium heatproof bowl, whisk eggs, sugar, and juice to blend. Set bowl over medium saucepan of simmering water. Whisk mixture constantly 5 minutes, or until light and fluffy and thick enough to coat back of spoon.

Remove bowl from over water and cool 5 minutes. Whisk in butter. Cover and refrigerate 1 hour, or until chilled and set.

*Serves 6*

*Make-Ahead*
These pancakes must be eaten as soon as they're made.

---

2 tbs
Unsalted butter, softened

6
Large eggs

¾ cup
Whole milk, lukewarm

¼ cup
Heavy cream, lukewarm

1
Lemon, zested

3 tbs
Unsalted butter, melted

¾ cup
Unbleached all-purpose flour, sifted

⅓ cup
Powdered sugar, plus more for dusting

¼ tsp
Kosher salt

1¼ cups
Vannessa's Lemon Butter (see recipe)

½ cup
Mascarpone cheese

Position rack in center of oven, allowing room for pancakes to rise, and preheat oven to 400°F.

Brush softened butter over two 8-inch round cake pans or 12 muffin cups to coat thickly and preheat pan in oven 3 minutes, or until very hot.

Meanwhile, in blender, blend eggs 1 minute, or until very frothy. With blender running, stream in milk, cream, lemon zest, and melted butter and blend 30 seconds. Add flour, sugar, and salt and blend until smooth batter forms.

Divide batter between hot pans. Bake 15 to 20 minutes if using cake pans or 12 minutes if using muffin pan, or until pancakes are puffed and brown around edges.

Transfer pancakes to plates and dust with powdered sugar. Serve immediately with lemon butter and dollops of mascarpone.

*Rochelle's Tip:*
These pancakes are pretty special with the lemon butter, but you can also serve them with your favorite jam or syrup.

# GERMAN PANCAKES

with Lemon Butter

Frozen Banana–Peanut Butter

# ICE CREAM CAKE for Dad

*Serves 12*

*Make-Ahead*
The cake, without the topping, can be made up to 2 weeks ahead; keep frozen.

7 oz
Bittersweet chocolate (70% cacao), melted, slightly warm, divided

1 tbs
Unsalted butter

6 oz
Chocolate wafer cookies (about 30)

4
Bananas

1/2 cup
Crunchy peanut butter

1 1/2 quarts
Good-quality vanilla ice cream, slightly softened

3/4 cup
Heavy cream, whipped to stiff peaks

2 tbs
Roasted peanuts, coarsely chopped (optional)

In small bowl set over simmering water, stir 3 oz melted chocolate and butter until blended. In food processor, grind cookies into very fine crumbs. Add chocolate-butter mixture and pinch of salt and pulse until moistened. Press crumb mixture evenly into 8-inch round cake pan. Freeze 10 minutes to harden crust.

Thickly slice 2 bananas. In large bowl, fold sliced bananas, peanut butter, and 4 oz melted chocolate into ice cream. Pour into crust and smooth top. Freeze cake 8 hours, or until hardened.

Invert cake onto plate. Turn cake right side up so crust is on bottom.

Spoon whipped cream over cake. Halve 2 bananas lengthwise and arrange bananas over cream. Sprinkle with peanuts, if desired, and serve.

"World-Famous"

# STICKY BUNS

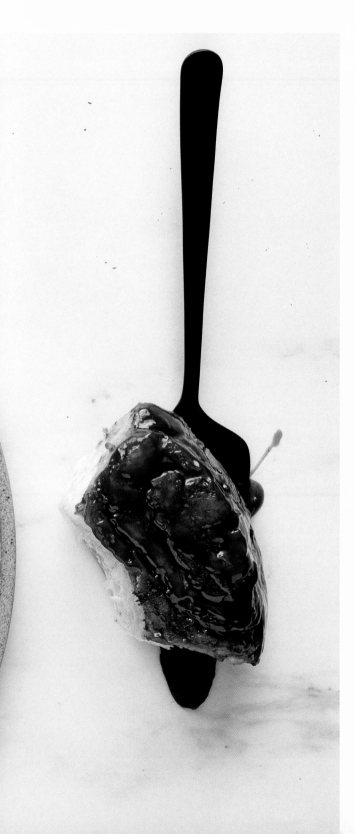

*Serves 12*

*Make-Ahead*
Buns can be arranged in pans, covered, and frozen up to 1 month. Allow extra time for dough to rise before baking.

---

*Honey Caramel Sauce:*

**¹⁄₂ cup**
Heavy cream

**¹⁄₂ cup**
Packed dark brown sugar

**6 tbs**
(¾ stick) Unsalted butter

**¹⁄₄ cup**
Honey

**¹⁄₄ tsp**
Kosher salt

*Buns:*

**1 recipe**
Butter-Layered Sweet Dough (page 78)

**6 tbs**
(¾ stick) Unsalted butter, softened

**1 cup**
Packed dark brown sugar

**2 tbs**
Ground cinnamon

*To make honey caramel sauce:*
In medium saucepan over medium heat, whisk cream, sugar, butter, honey, and salt 3 minutes, or until blended. Pour sauce into two 8-inch round cake pans, two 9-inch square baking pans, or 13x9-inch baking pan. Cool.

*Meanwhile, to make buns:*
Roll out dough to 17x13-inch rectangle. Spread butter over dough, leaving ¹⁄₂-inch plain border along top edge of dough.

Mix brown sugar and cinnamon; sprinkle over butter and pat to adhere.

Beginning with long edge nearest to you, roll dough into tight cylinder. Firmly pinch seam to seal. Position seam side down.

Slide unflavored dental floss under roll and crisscross over roll to cut into 12 pieces. Place buns, cut side down, over caramel in pans. Cover and place in warm area 45 minutes, or until buns double in size.

Meanwhile, place sheet of foil on lower oven rack to catch any caramel drippings and position another rack in center of oven; preheat to 325°F. Bake on center rack 35 minutes, or until buns are golden brown and baked through. Cool 5 minutes. Invert onto platters and serve.

Butter-Layered

# SWEET DOUGH

*Makes*
2½ lb

*Make-Ahead*
Dough can be stored airtight and frozen up to
1 month. Thaw in refrigerator before using.

---

**½ cup**
Warm water

**2 tsp + 3 tbs**
Sugar

**1 tbs**
Dry yeast

**3 cups**
Unbleached all-
purpose flour, plus
more for dusting

**1½ tsp**
Kosher salt

**¾ cup**
Whole milk, room
temperature

**3**
Large egg yolks

**12 tbs**
(1½ sticks)
Unsalted butter,
softened, divided

In 2-cup measuring cup, stir water, 2 tsp sugar, and yeast. Let stand 5 minutes, or until foamy.

Using electric stand mixer with hook attachment, mix flour, 3 tbs sugar, and salt in mixer bowl. Add milk, yolks, and yeast mixture and mix 2 minutes on medium speed, or until dough forms.

Gradually beat in 4 tbs butter. Mix on medium-low speed 5 minutes, or until dough is smooth, elastic, and slightly sticky. Cover and chill 45 minutes.

Roll out dough on lightly floured surface to 16x12-inch rectangle. Brush off excess flour. Spread 8 tbs butter over left two-thirds of dough, leaving 1-inch plain border.

Fold unbuttered portion over center third, then fold remaining buttered third over folded two-thirds, as is done for folding letters. Place on lightly floured sheet pan. Cover and chill 1 hour.

Roll out dough on floured work surface to 16x12-inch rectangle. Repeat letter fold and chill dough on sheet pan 1 hour. Repeat this rolling, folding, and chilling process 2 more times.

# RICE PILAF

## with Garbanzos and Brown Butter

*Serves 4*

*Make-Ahead*
Can be made 1 day ahead; cover and refrigerate. Rewarm before serving.

**1 ½ cups**
Boiling chicken stock

**1 cup**
Uncooked long-grain white rice

**¼ cup**
Finely chopped onion

**1 clove**
Garlic, finely chopped

**¾ tsp**
Kosher salt

**⅛ tsp**
Ground black pepper

**4 tbs**
(½ stick) Butter, melted, divided

**1 cup**
Drained canned garbanzo beans

**1 tbs**
Chopped fresh cilantro

Lemon wedges, for serving

Preheat oven to 375°F. In 8-inch round cake pan, combine boiling stock, rice, onion, garlic, salt, and pepper. Stir in 2 tbs melted butter. Cover and bake 30 minutes, or until rice is tender. Fluff rice with fork.

Meanwhile, in large skillet, sauté garbanzo beans with 2 tbs butter over medium heat until heated through and butter browns.

Spoon beans over rice. Sprinkle with cilantro and serve with lemon wedges.

*Makes*
12 bars

*Make-Ahead*
The bars, without their meringue topping, can be made up to 2 days ahead; wrap in plastic and store at room temperature.

8 tbs
(1 stick) Unsalted butter, softened, divided

2 cups
Graham cracker crumbs, divided

2 tbs + 1/2 cup
Granulated sugar, divided

1 tbs
Unbleached all-purpose flour

1 1/4 cups
Packed golden brown sugar

2
Large eggs

2 tsp
Vanilla extract

1/2 tsp
Salt

1/4 tsp
Baking powder

2/3 cup
Pecans, chopped

1/3 cup
Dark chocolate chunks

3
Large egg whites

Preheat oven to 350°F. Brush 2 tbs butter over 9-inch square baking pan or 8-inch round cake pan.

In large bowl, using electric mixer on medium-high speed, beat 1 1/2 cups graham cracker crumbs, 6 tbs butter, 2 tbs granulated sugar, and flour until moist. Press firmly and evenly over bottom of pan. Bake 10 minutes, or until crust is golden brown.

In large bowl, whisk brown sugar, eggs, vanilla, salt, baking powder, and 1/2 cup graham cracker crumbs to blend. Stir in pecans and chocolate. Spread over baked crust and bake 22 minutes, or until filling is dark golden on top and moves slightly when pan is gently shaken. Transfer pan to rack and cool completely.

Transfer bar to platter.

In medium bowl, using electric mixer on medium-high speed, beat egg whites until foamy. Gradually add 1/2 cup granulated sugar and beat 4 minutes, or until firm glossy peaks form. Dollop meringue decoratively over bar.

Cut bar into 12 pieces. Using kitchen blowtorch, torch meringue until browned and serve.

# CAMPFIRE BARS

# POTATO GRATIN

with **Creamy Thyme Sauce**

*Serves 8 - 10*

*Make-Ahead*
This gratin is best eaten while still warm and saucy.

**3 lb**
Russet or Yukon Gold potatoes, peeled, cut into ⅛-inch-thick slices

**2 cloves**
garlic, finely chopped

**1 tbs**
Fresh thyme leaves

**3 cups**
Heavy cream

**8 oz**
Gruyère cheese, grated

Preheat oven to 350°F.

Arrange one-fourth of potatoes over 13x9-inch baking pan or two 8-inch round cake pans, overlapping slices slightly and forming 1 layer. Sprinkle with one-fourth each of garlic and thyme; season with salt and pepper. Drizzle over one-fourth of cream, then sprinkle with one-fourth of cheese. Repeat to form 4 layers total.

Bake uncovered 50 to 55 minutes, or until potatoes are just tender and gratin is golden brown on top. Cool slightly and serve.

*Serves 6*

*Make-Ahead*
The meatloaf mixture can be made up to
1 day ahead; cover and refrigerate.

---

**1 1/2 cups**
Cubed (1/2-inch)
French baguette

**1/2 cup**
Whole milk

**2 1/2 lb**
Ground beef (80%
lean)

**1/2 cup**
Finely chopped fresh
parsley

**1/2 cup**
Coarsely grated
onion (use large
holes on box grater)

**1 cup**
Freshly grated
Parmesan cheese,
plus more for
serving

**1/2 cup**
Tomato paste

**3**
Large eggs, beaten
to blend

**1 tbs**
Finely grated garlic

**2 tsp**
Chopped fresh thyme

**1 tsp**
Crushed red pepper
flakes (optional)

**1 1/2 cups**
Simple Marinara
Sauce (page 36) or
purchased

Position rack in middle of oven
and preheat oven to 350°F. Set
perforated meatloaf insert in
9x5x3-inch loaf pan.

In large bowl, stir bread cubes and
milk. Soak 10 minutes, or until
bread is very soft. Mash bread with
your hands.

Mix beef, parsley, onion, Parmesan,
tomato paste, eggs, garlic, thyme,
red pepper flakes, and 1 tbs salt into
bread mixture. Transfer to loaf pan.

Bake 45 minutes. Remove pan from
oven. Lift perforated insert with
meatloaf and set aside. Pour off excess
liquid. Return insert with meatloaf to
pan and continue baking 15 minutes,
or until instant-read thermometer
inserted into center of loaf reads
150°F. Lift meatloaf from pan and
slide onto carving board. Rest 10
minutes. Serve with marinara sauce
and more Parmesan cheese.

*Rochelle's Tip:*
I also like to serve this meatloaf
as "meatball" sandwiches. Tuck
warm slices of meatloaf into
toasted French rolls, and smother
with marinara sauce. Top with
mozzarella and Parmesan cheese
and broil until mozzarella is melted
and gooey.

# MEATBALL MEATLOAF

with **Marinara**

# CORNBREAD CAKE

with Berries and Cream

*Serves 8 - 10*

*Make-Ahead*
Cake can be made up to 1 day ahead; store airtight in refrigerator. Bring to room temperature before serving.

³/₄ cup
Unbleached all-purpose flour

²/₃ cup
Yellow cornmeal

1 tbs
Baking powder

1 cup
(2 sticks) Unsalted butter, softened

1 cup
Granulated sugar

2 tsp
Orange zest (optional)

¹/₂ tsp
Kosher salt

2
Large egg yolks

4
Large eggs, separated

6 oz
Fresh blackberries

*Accompaniments:*
Powdered sugar, whipped cream, fresh raspberries

Preheat oven to 350°F. Lightly butter 9x5x3-inch loaf pan or 8-inch round cake pan.

In medium bowl, whisk flour, cornmeal, and baking powder. In large bowl, using electric mixer on medium-high speed, beat butter, sugar, zest, if using, and salt until light and fluffy. Beat in 6 yolks 1 at a time. Stir in cornmeal mixture.

In clean large bowl, using electric mixer with whisk attachment on medium-high speed, beat 4 egg whites until stiff peaks form. Stir half of whites into batter to lighten it, then fold in remaining whites.

Spoon about one-fourth of batter into pan. Sprinkle blackberries over batter. Top with remaining batter.

Bake 50 minutes, or until tester inserted into center comes out clean and top is dark golden brown. Rest 15 minutes. Invert cake onto platter and cool.

Dust cake with powdered sugar, cut into slices or wedges, and serve with whipped cream and raspberries.

*Rochelle's Tip:*
When I serve this cake to my Italian family and friends, I call it Polenta Cake. Feel free to adapt the recipe titles to best suit your crowd.

# MUFFIN PANS
## AND POPOVER
## PANS

*Makes 12*

*Make-Ahead*
These cakes are best
enjoyed while still warm.

**10 oz**
Semisweet
chocolate (60%
cacao), chopped

**12 tbs**
(1½ sticks)
Unsalted butter

**4**
Large eggs

**6 tbs**
Sugar

Nonstick cooking
spray

**1 quart**
Vanilla ice cream,
for serving

**¼ cup**
Freeze-dried
raspberries,
ground into
powder

Preheat oven to 325°F. In small
saucepan over low heat, stir
chocolate and butter constantly
until melted. Stir in pinch of salt.
Remove from heat and cool slightly.

In large bowl, using electric
handheld mixer, beat eggs and sugar
4 minutes, or until pale and thick.
Fold in cooled chocolate mixture.

Spray 12 muffin cups lightly with
nonstick cooking spray. Divide
batter among muffin cups and
bake 12 minutes, or until cakes are
puffed around edges with moist
centers. Cool 2 minutes. Invert
cakes onto platter, then transfer
cakes to plates.

Spoon small scoop of ice cream
alongside cakes. Dust with
raspberry powder and serve.

*Rochelle's Tip:*
Use a clean coffee grinder to
pulverize the freeze-dried
raspberries into a powder. The
powder works well as a pretty
finishing touch (these cakes
are just one example) or as an
all-natural way to color your
frostings—check out my Girly Pink
Sheet Cake (page 24) to see how.

Raspberry-Dusted Flourless

# CHOCOLATE CAKES

Ricotta-Citrus

# STREUSEL MUFFINS

*Makes 12*

*Make-Ahead*
The streusel topping can be made up to 5 days ahead; cover and freeze.

**2 ¹/₄ cups**
Unbleached all-purpose flour, divided

**¹/₃ cup + ³/₄ cup**
Sugar, divided

**²/₃ cup**
Sliced almonds

**4 tbs**
(½ stick) Chilled unsalted butter

**13 tbs**
Unsalted butter, softened, divided

**1 ¹/₄ tsp**
Baking powder

**³/₄ tsp**
Baking soda

**¹/₂ tsp**
Salt

**1 ¹/₂ tsp each**
Finely grated lemon zest, orange zest, and lime zest

**1 ¹/₄ cups**
Whole-milk ricotta cheese

**2**
Large eggs

**¹/₂ tsp**
Almond extract

*To make streusel topping:*
In medium bowl, mix ¹/₂ cup flour, ¹/₃ cup sugar, and almonds to blend. Using fingers, rub chilled butter into flour mixture until moist clumps form. Chill until needed.

*To make muffins:*
Preheat oven to 350°F. Brush 12 muffin cups with 1 tbs softened butter. In small bowl, whisk 1 ³/₄ cups flour, baking powder, baking soda, and salt to blend.

In large bowl, using electric mixer on medium-high speed, beat ³/₄ cup sugar, 12 tbs softened butter, and zests until fluffy. Beat in ricotta, eggs, and almond extract. Beat in flour mixture.

Divide batter among prepared muffin cups. Sprinkle streusel topping over and bake 30 minutes, or until golden on top. Cool slightly. Serve warm.

*Makes 12*

*Make-Ahead*
These cakes can be made up to 1 day ahead; store
in an airtight container at room temperature.

*Cakes:*

**8 tbs**
(1 stick) Unsalted
butter, softened,
plus more for
coating pan

**2 cups**
Unbleached cake
flour

**1 1/4 tsp**
Baking powder

**3/4 tsp**
Baking soda

**3/4 tsp**
Salt

**1 cup**
Sugar

**1 1/2 tsp**
Vanilla extract

**2**
Large eggs

**1 cup**
Sour cream

**5 tsp**
Instant espresso
powder, plus more
for garnish

**1 tsp**
Ground cinnamon,
plus more for
garnish

*Espresso Glaze:*

**2 tbs**
Instant espresso
powder

**2 cups**
Powdered sugar,
sifted

*To prepare cakes:*
Preheat oven to 350°F. Brush 12
muffin cups with butter.

In medium bowl, whisk flour,
baking powder, baking soda, and
salt. In large bowl, using electric
mixer on medium-high speed, beat
sugar, butter, and vanilla until
fluffy. Mix in eggs 1 at a time. Mix
in sour cream. Add flour mixture
and mix just until blended.

In another medium bowl, mix
espresso powder and cinnamon with
1 tbs hot water. Stir half of batter
(about 2 cups) into espresso mixture.

Drop batters alternately into muffin
cups. Swirl batters with skewer.

Bake 16 to 18 minutes, or until tester
inserted in center of cakes comes
out with some crumbs attached.
Cool pan on rack 5 minutes.
Transfer cakes to rack and cool.

*To glaze cakes:*
In small bowl, whisk 3 tbs hot water
and espresso powder. Add sugar and
whisk until smooth. Dip tops of
cakes into glaze. Sprinkle with pinch
of espresso powder and cinnamon.

Glazed
# ESPRESSO
# CAKES

Croissant French Toast

# SOUFFLÉS

*Makes 12*

*Make-Ahead*
The custard can be made up to 2 days ahead; cover and refrigerate.

2 tbs
Unsalted butter, softened

¾ cup
Heavy cream

¾ cup
Whole milk

5
Large eggs

2 tbs
Sugar, plus more for sprinkling

1
Vanilla bean, split lengthwise, or 2 tsp vanilla extract

12
Small or 3 large croissants, cut into 1-inch pieces

Pure maple syrup, for serving

Preheat oven to 400°F. Brush 12 muffin cups with butter.

In large bowl, whisk cream, milk, eggs, and sugar to blend. Scrape seeds from vanilla bean into custard (reserve bean for another use) or add vanilla extract.

Arrange croissants in muffin cups. Divide custard among cups. Soak croissants until saturated. Sprinkle with sugar.

Bake 10 to 12 minutes, or until puffed and golden brown. Transfer soufflés to plates. Drizzle with maple syrup and serve.

*Rochelle's Tip:*
If you like, you can save a scraped vanilla bean for a variety of other uses, such as cooking it with your oatmeal or rice pudding, or infusing granulated sugar.

*Makes 12*

*Make-Ahead*
The filling can be made 1 day ahead;
cover and refrigerate.

9 oz
Feta cheese,
crumbled

9 oz
Fontina or Havarti
cheese, shredded

3/4 cup
Chopped baby kale

3/4 cup
Chopped fresh
parsley

3/4 cup
Heavy cream

6
Large egg yolks

3 tbs
Minced shallot

10
14x9-inch sheets
phyllo pastry,
thawed if frozen

5 tbs
Butter, melted

Place rack in lowest position of
oven; preheat to 375°F.

In medium bowl, mix cheeses, kale,
parsley, cream, yolks, and shallot.

Place 1 phyllo sheet on work
surface and brush with butter.
Top with another phyllo sheet.
Repeat stacking 3 more phyllo
sheets, brushing each with butter.
Cut phyllo stack into six 4 1/2-
inch squares. Line muffin cups
with phyllo squares. Repeat with
remaining phyllo and butter,
lining 12 cups total. Divide cheese
mixture among phyllo cups.

Bake 20 minutes, or until golden
brown on bottom. Transfer to rack
to cool 5 minutes before serving.

Kale and Parsley

# SPANAKOPITA TARTS

Beer-Braised

# MUSHROOM HAND PIES

*Makes 12*

*Make-Ahead*
The mushroom mixture can be made
1 day ahead; cover and refrigerate.

---

4
Medium shallots,
quartered

4 cloves
Garlic

3 tbs
Fresh thyme
leaves

2 lb
White mushrooms

8 tbs
(1 stick) Butter

1 $\frac{1}{2}$ cups
Blond ale

3 sheets
Frozen puff pastry,
cut into twelve
4½-inch squares

1
Egg, beaten to
blend

Flaky sea salt

Preheat oven to 425°F.

In food processor, mince shallots, garlic, and thyme. Transfer to large bowl.

Working in 5 batches, add mushrooms to processor and pulse to chop very coarsely.

In large nonstick skillet over medium-high heat, melt butter. Add shallot mixture and mushrooms and cook 25 minutes, or until mushrooms are golden brown. Add ale and cook 7 minutes. Remove from heat. Season with salt and pepper. Cool completely.

Line 12 muffin cups with pastry squares. Divide mushroom mixture among pastries, pressing into cups. Brush pastry tips with egg. Fold in tips and press to seal. Brush pastry with egg and sprinkle with sea salt. Bake 25 to 30 minutes, or until golden brown on bottom.

*Makes 12*

*Make-Ahead*
These are best eaten warm from the oven, but can be covered and refrigerated up to 2 days; rewarm them in the microwave.

6
Hatch chiles or Anaheim chiles

2 tsp
Olive oil

2 tbs
Butter, softened

6 oz
Monterey Jack cheese, grated (about 2 cups)

7
Large eggs

3/4 cup
Whole milk

1/2 cup
Heavy cream

*Accompaniments:*
Sour cream, cilantro, sliced green onions

Preheat oven to 450°F. Coat chiles with oil on sheet pan. Roast chiles, turning as needed, for 25 minutes, or until blistered all over and beginning to brown. Cover with towel and cool 10 minutes. Peel, seed, and coarsely chop chiles.

Decrease oven temperature to 300°F. Brush 12 muffin cups with butter. Divide chiles and cheese among muffin cups.

In large bowl, whisk eggs, milk, and cream to blend. Season with 1/2 tsp salt. Divide among muffin cups.

Bake 15 minutes, or until mixture is almost set in center. Cool 5 minutes. Transfer to plates and serve with accompaniments.

*Rochelle's Tip:*
You can replace the roasted chopped chiles with any cooked vegetable, and you can swap out the Jack cheese for your favorite cheese. I also like making these bites with sliced grilled zucchini and onions and feta cheese.

# EGG BITES

with **Hatch Chiles** and **Monterey Jack**

Pineapple-Lime
# ICE POPS

*Makes*
6 large or 12 small
ice pops

*Make-Ahead*
Can be made 1 week ahead;
keep frozen.

---

1
Medium pineapple,
peeled

3
Limes, zested
(about 1½ tbs),
juiced (about
½ cup)

$^1/_2$ cup
Agave syrup

6 to 12
Ice-pop sticks

Cut six or twelve $^1/_4$-inch-thick round slices from top end of pineapple. Using 2 $^3/_4$-inch-diameter cookie cutter, cut out 1 disk from each slice, keeping core in center. Reserve trimmings (about 1 cup for 6 pops or 2 cups for 12 pops). Insert ice-pop sticks through core of each disk and set aside.

Coarsely chop remaining pineapple (about 2 cups for 6 pops or 3 cups for 12 pops) and transfer to blender. Add pineapple trimmings, lime juice, 1 tbs lime zest, and 1 cup water and blend until smooth. Strain into pitcher. Stir in agave, $^1/_2$ tbs lime zest, and pinch of salt. Divide mixture among 6 popover cups or 12 muffin cups.

Set pineapple rounds atop cups so stick is submerged through cup. Freeze overnight.

Wrap each cup with hot wet kitchen towel for a few seconds, then wiggle ice pops to loosen and remove. Enjoy immediately or wrap ice pops in plastic and keep frozen.

*Rochelle's Tip:*
Keep these ice pops on hand to turn into a frozen margarita. Remove the ice-pop stick from 1 large pineapple-lime pop or 2 smaller pops. Blend with 2 tbs silver tequila and 1 cup ice cubes until smooth and icy. Pour into a glass and enjoy!

*Makes*
6 large or 12
small popovers

*Make-Ahead*
These must be eaten
hot from the oven.

---

1 1/2 tbs
Unsalted butter,
softened

1 1/2 cups
Whole milk, room
temperature

4
Large eggs, room
temperature

1 2/3 cups
Unbleached all-
purpose flour, sifted

1 1/4 tsp
Kosher salt

1 1/2 tbs
Unsalted butter,
melted

Position rack in center of oven,
allowing enough room above rack
for popovers to rise, and preheat
oven to 425°F.

Brush softened butter thickly over
6 cups of popover pan or 12 cups of
muffin pan and preheat pan in oven
for 3 minutes, or until very hot.

Meanwhile, in blender, blend milk,
eggs, flour, salt, and melted butter
to form smooth thin batter.

Divide batter among cups of hot
pan and immediately return to
oven. Bake 35 minutes, or until
popovers are puffed and deep
golden brown. Serve immediately.

*Rochelle's Tip:*
A classic accompaniment to prime
rib. And don't forget the Crunchy
Roasted Potatoes (page 31).

Crisp and Custardy

# POPOVERS

# INDEX

# Rochelle Palermo

Rochelle Palermo is the Vice President of Culinary Operations for Stone's Food, Inc., overseeing all culinary operations and content for chef Curtis Stone. She has been Stone's right hand in the kitchen since his arrival in the United States, at various times serving as his culinary producer, food consultant, product developer, food editor, food stylist, recipe developer, and tester for television, cookbooks, magazines, live appearances, and products. She helped Stone write his *New York Times* best-selling cookbook, *What's for Dinner?*, as well as *Good Food, Good Life* and *Relaxed Cooking with Curtis Stone*. She now works with him on his brand of cookware, cooking tools, and appliances for the Home Shopping Network (HSN) and The Shopping Channel (TSC) in Canada, where she alternately provides behind-the-scenes support and appears as on-air talent.

*@rochellepalermo*

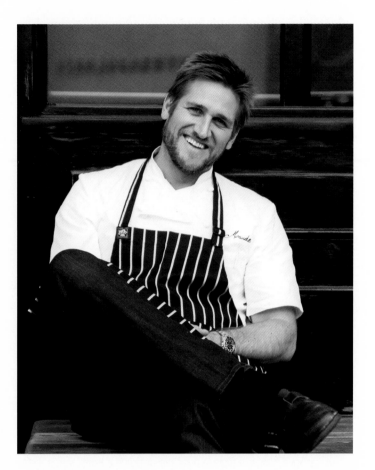

## Curtis Stone

Curtis Stone is chef-owner of the award-winning restaurants
Maude in Beverly Hills and Gwen Butcher Shop & Restaurant
in Hollywood and a *New York Times* best-selling author of six
cookbooks. He has hosted a number of top-rated programs
including *Take Home Chef* and *The Rachael Ray Show,* as well as
several popular shows across the *Top Chef* franchise and Food
Network. In 2007, Stone developed Kitchen Solutions, a premium
cookware range that solves the common problems home cooks face
every day. More recently, he launched his Dura-Bake line. Born
in Melbourne, Australia, Stone now lives in Los Angeles with his
wife, actress Lindsay Price, and their two young sons.

*curtisstone.com*     *@curtisstone*

Published in the United States of America by
Stone's Food, Inc.

Photographs © Ray Kachatorian

Printed in the United States of America

First Edition, first printing
Printed by Franklin Press Incorporated

Book and Cover Design by Nathan Hinz
Production Design by Tracy Hogenson
Photography by Ray Kachatorian
Copyediting by Amy Steinberg
Food Styling by Vivian Lui
Assistant Food Styling by
Matthew Glasser, Vannessa Garcia,
Jenifer Gomez, and Avette Aumentado
Prop Styling by Suzie Myers

ISBN: 978-0-692-96532-0